CAPTURED
TELEVISION
HISTORY

TV LAUNCHES
24-HOUR NEWS WITH CNN

An Augmented Reading Experience

By Michael Burgan

Content Adviser: Alan Schroeder, Professor,
School of Journalism, Northeastern University

COMPASS POINT BOOKS
a capstone imprint

Compass Point Books are published by Capstone Press,
1710 Roe Crest Drive, North Mankato, Minnesota 56003
www.mycapstone.com

Editorial Credits
Michelle Bisson, editor; Tracy McCabe, designer; Svetlana Zhurkin, media researcher;
Katy LaVigne, production specialist

Photo Credits
Alamy: Barry King, 29, Tina Manley, 5; AP Photo: 8, Beth A. Keiser, 22, D. Mollard, 15, Ric Feld,
44, 59 (top left); Getty Images: AFP/Georges Rumens, 33, CNN, 7, 14, 57 (bottom), 58 (top),
Dario Mitidieri, 13, Fotosearch, 43, Fox News Channel, 45, Gamma-Rapho/1020, 48, Kaveh
Kazemi, 32, 36, Liaison/Cynthia Johnson, 25, 56, Paul Hawthorne, cover, 27, The LIFE Images
Collection/Allan Tannenbaum, 40, The LIFE Images Collection/Ted Thai, 37; Granger, 17, 18, 57
(top); Newscom: Dennis Brack, 6, Reuters/Lucas Jackson, 53, Reuters/Mike Segar, 47, 59 (top
right), Reuters/Patrick de Noirmont, 11, Sipa Press/Charlie Varley, 50, Splash News/Photo Image
Press, 52, Zuma Press/Cheryl Hatch, 41, Zuma Press/Nina Prommer, 35; Shutterstock: Evan
El-Amin, 59 (bottom), s_bukley, 58 (bottom); Wikimedia: NASA, 20

Library of Congress Cataloging-in-Publication Data
Library of Congress Cataloging-in-Publication Data
Names: Burgan, Michael, author.
Title: TV launches 24-hour news with CNN / by Michael Burgan.
Description: North Mankato, Minnesota : Compass Point Books, [2020] |
Audience: Ages 10-12. | Audience: Grades 4-6. | Includes bibliographical
references and index
Identifiers: LCCN 2018054584| ISBN 9780756560003 (hardcover)
ISBN 9780756560041 (paperback) | ISBN 9780756560089 (ebook pdf)
Subjects: LCSH: Cable News Network—History—Juvenile literature. |
Television broadcasting of news—United States—Juvenile literature.
Classification: LCC PN4888.T4 B87 2020 | DDC 384.5506/573--dc23
LC record available at https://lccn.loc.gov/2018054584

All internet sites appearing in the back matter were available and accurate when this book
was sent to press.

Download the Capstone app!

- Ask an adult to download the Capstone 4D app.

- Scan the cover and stars inside the book for additional content.

When you scan a spread, you'll find fun extra stuff
to go with this book! You can also find these things
on the web at www.capstone4D.com using the
password: CNN.60003

Printed and bound in the USA.
PA017

TABLEOFCONTENTS

Chapter One

BRINGING A WAR TO THE WORLD

Bernard Shaw looked out the window of his room on the ninth floor of Baghdad's Al-Rashid Hotel. Shaw was the main anchor for the Cable News Network (CNN), which broadcast news around the world 24 hours a day. With him in the hotel suite were two CNN reporters—Peter Arnett and John Holliman—and other CNN staff.

The CNN team had been sent to Baghdad, the capital of Iraq, to report on the growing threat of war in the region. Just over five months earlier, on August 2, 1990, Iraqi leader Saddam Hussein had sent his army into neighboring Kuwait. Hussein invaded, in part, because he didn't want to repay money he had borrowed from the Kuwaiti government. His army quickly seized control of Kuwait.

In the United States, President George H.W. Bush responded to the invasion by assembling an international military force to drive the Iraqis out of Kuwait. The United Nations warned Hussein that this force would attack if Iraqi troops did not leave Kuwait by January 15, 1991. The deadline had passed just hours before. Now the reporters waited in their hotel room for the attack on Iraq to begin.

The Al-Rashid Hotel served as the base for CNN reporters during the war in Iraq.

U.S. troops were sent to Saudi Arabia in 1990 to combat the invasion of Iraq.

CNN had been preparing to cover a possible war in Iraq for months. It was the world's only 24-hour news channel. The cable network was barely 10 years old, and many people in the media still thought it did not match the best reporting done by the major U.S. television networks, sometimes called the "Big Three"—CBS, NBC, and ABC. These networks had existed for decades. But CNN owner Ted Turner was determined to become the leader in televised news in the United States and around the world. He hired Tom Johnson as network president on August 1, 1990.

Bernard Shaw
interviewed
Saddam Hussein
shortly before the
war in Iraq began.

As CNN prepared to report on events in Iraq and Kuwait, Johnson asked Turner how much he could spend. Turner said, "You spend whatever you think it takes, pal." With Turner's permission, Johnson eventually spent more than $20 million to cover the war, sending reporters across the Middle East.

Shaw had first gone to Baghdad in October 1990 to interview Hussein. Earlier, CNN's international division had televised a statement Hussein had recorded, explaining why Iraq had a right to invade Kuwait. In the U.S., CNN showed videos of hostages the Iraqis had taken after the invasion. In the videos produced by Iraq, Hussein claimed Iraq was treating the hostages well. CNN did not question his statement or ask for proof that the hostages were being treated well. Some media experts criticized CNN for airing propaganda that served Hussein's interests. CNN

Iraqi TV Taped Broadcast   CNN LIVE

CNN aired footage of Saddam Hussein meeting with the hostages Iraq had taken.

said it considered the videos true news coverage. However, when it aired the next video Hussein had made, it ran a disclaimer in the crawl that said "Live video provided by Iraqi TV." This meant that the images came from the Iraqi government, not CNN's own camera crews. Essentially, they admitted they couldn't verify what they were showing, but that it was all the available footage.

Because the threat of war was so close, Shaw had come back to Baghdad in January 1991 to try to interview Hussein again. He and CNN believed that Americans needed to hear the Iraqi view of events, especially with war likely to break out. This time, however, Hussein was too busy to meet with Shaw.

Then, on January 16, White House spokesman Marlin Fitzwater warned CNN that it should pull out of Baghdad. Some reporters from the U.S. and Europe had already begun to leave the city. Fitzwater told Tom Johnson that the lives of his reporters and crew were in danger.

Johnson considered what to do. When he was publisher of the *Los Angeles Times*, two of his reporters had died while covering international conflicts. Should he risk the lives of the CNN team in Baghdad? Johnson discussed the situation with Ted Turner. Turner said, "I will take on myself the responsibility for anybody who is killed. I'll take it off of you . . ." Johnson was still thinking he should pull out the crew. The two men finally agreed to let the reporters and others decide what to do.

Back in Baghdad the CNN staff discussed whether they should leave. CNN had a plane waiting for them in the neighboring country of Jordan—that was assuming they could reach the plane before fighting began. Some people in the city thought President Bush might delay an attack. Ingrid Formanek, a CNN producer at the Al-Rashid Hotel, knew the team members wanted to do their job—to report on whatever happened next in Iraq. But they also knew the danger they faced. As she wrote years later, "We'd wake up in the morning feeling brave [and] get scared by lunchtime . . ." In his report on January 16,

Shaw told CNN viewers he was planning to leave the next day, "and I leave Baghdad very disappointed that I have not accomplished the mission that I had." Yet as January 17 began in Baghdad, Shaw was still there with others, not sure if he could leave, despite the plan to do so.

As part of its preparations for covering the war, CNN had struck a deal with Iraq. Hussein agreed to give the network its own direct phone line out of Iraq. No other TV network had this. Formanek thought that the Iraqis wanted to listen in secretly. They assumed CNN reporters might receive or share information that would help Iraq during a war. Formanek later wrote, "The Iraqis really thought we knew more than we did, and they hoped to learn what the Bush Administration was thinking and planning."

With the separate phone line, if bombs fell on Baghdad and knocked out the regular phone system, CNN could still give live audio reports. Meanwhile, Shaw waited with the rest of the world to see if the international force would carry out its threat. Would it attack Iraq because Hussein had not pulled his troops out of Kuwait by the UN deadline?

The answer came with a quiet flutter. Shaw looked out the hotel window and saw pieces of silver metal falling through the sky. He realized they had been dropped by Allied planes to confuse Iraq's radar systems. Dogs barked outside the hotel, as if they

"The Iraqis really thought we knew more than we did, and they hoped to learn what the Bush Administration was thinking and planning."

sensed something was about to happen. Then a huge colored light burst across the sky. Guns began to go off around the hotel, and air-raid sirens blared, warning people to take shelter. It was about 2:32 a.m. local time, and eight hours earlier in the eastern United States.

Shaw reached for the microphone and the special phone connection to CNN headquarters in Atlanta. He said, "Something is happening outside. Peter Arnett, join me here. Let's describe to our viewers what we're seeing. The skies over Baghdad have been illuminated. We're seeing bright flashes going off all over the sky." In the U.S., viewers saw a picture of Shaw placed over a map of Iraq as he gave his audio report; no video image was available. Since CNN only had a direct phone line

Antiaircraft fire and tracer flares lit up the sky above Baghdad on January 17, 1991.

to Iraq, the lack of video was not surprising. What was surprising was having a real-time, unedited description of an attack.

Shaw then turned the microphone over to Arnett, who told viewers that antiaircraft gunfire was going off around the hotel. "We hear the sounds of planes, they're coming over our hotel; however, we have not yet heard the sound of bombs." A few minutes later, John Holliman took the microphone and dangled it out the window so CNN viewers could better hear the first sounds of the war.

Other networks reported this first military activity over Baghdad, but ABC and NBC lost live contact with their reporters soon after the actual bombing started. Eventually CBS also lost contact, as the U.S.–led attack knocked out communication lines. But CNN's four-wire system let Shaw, Arnett, and Holliman continue to describe what they saw and heard through the night. CNN's exclusive reporting led some NBC and CBS affiliates to switch to CNN's coverage, and NBC ended up interviewing CNN reporters to give its viewers a sense of what was happening.

The network also received a boost when U.S. Secretary of Defense Dick Cheney said he was following the events in Baghdad by watching CNN. Other world leaders did so too. CNN reported without interruption, while the other networks sometimes cut to commercials. At one point, people watching ABC

THE TECHNOLOGY THAT MADE CNN FAMOUS

CNN's young staff worked with new technology to make sure that CNN's broadcasts were heard worldwide.

CNN and other news networks relied on satellites to broadcast images and words around the world. But it was a fairly simple bit of telephone technology that made CNN's reputation at the start of the fighting in Baghdad. All the networks sometimes used what was called a four-wire phone system. It had two pairs of phone lines, with one pair carrying sound from reporters to the United States and the other sending audio in the other direction. The extra lines provided better sound quality and let producers talk to their reporters as they were on the air. The system did not need to go through local phone companies, so major TV networks used a four-wire in parts of the world where local phones were not reliable.

Though all four U.S. networks tried to get a four-wire set up in Baghdad, only CNN succeeded. CNN had started asking the Iraqis to let their network use the system months before. Reporters at other networks thought Hussein favored CNN because it showed some of the video footage he wanted to air. He could follow that coverage because he could watch CNN's reporting with a satellite hookup. He did not have the same direct access to what the other U.S. networks aired. During the January 1991 bombing, CNN's four-wire sent audio to Amman, Jordan. From there, the sound was sent by satellite to CNN in Atlanta, Georgia. Without the four-wire, CNN could not have carried the first hours of the war live.

This map is what CNN viewers saw as Shaw reported on the first night of the Gulf War.

saw an ad for deodorant, while CNN viewers heard Shaw and the CNN team describe an attack by planes soaring over their hotel.

In Baghdad the bombing raid stopped for a bit. Some of the CNN crew headed for a bomb shelter, but the three reporters and several others remained in the hotel room. The bombing began again. Holliman described what he saw and heard: "Now there's a huge fire that we've just seen due west of our position. And we just heard—whoa. Holy cow. That was a large airburst we saw." The CNN team was convinced that the bombs falling around them had taken out their communications link with Atlanta. Holliman asked if the people at CNN headquarters could still hear them. A voice replied, "John, we do still hear you." And so could the rest of the world. CNN continued to

Smoke rose over Baghdad when the U.S. bombed it during Operation Desert Storm.

broadcast the only live reporting of the opening hours of what would be called the Gulf War.

The U.S. military referred to the fighting as Operation Desert Storm. It lasted six weeks, with the United States and its allies successfully forcing Iraqi troops out of Kuwait. CNN won international attention for its coverage, especially on the first night of the war. In the U.S. more than 11 million people watched that early reporting—many more than had ever before watched the network at any one time. With the Gulf War CNN proved that its 24-hour news reporting could play a huge role in immediately sharing important information around the world.

ChapterTwo
BUILDING A TV EMPIRE

Without the Atlanta Braves baseball team, CNN's Bernard Shaw (generally called "Bernie"), Peter Arnett, and the rest of the crew may never have been in Baghdad at the start of the Gulf War. In 1973, seven years before the launch of CNN, Ted Turner paid to begin airing Braves baseball games on the TV station he owned in Atlanta. The deal was a big one at the time. That was because Turner's Channel 17 had limited range compared to a much larger Atlanta station that had carried the games in the past. Turner wanted the Braves to be a featured part of his station's programming.

Turner first expanded the range of his station's reach by using microwaves, a form of energy that can be used to transmit radio and TV signals over long distances. The signal can be bounced from one tower to another, using antennas that send and receive the TV signal. But the signal can't go through obstacles such as buildings, so the towers are usually set on hills. Turner built a system of tall towers that carried Channel 17 to viewers in five southern states. Some received the signal with a TV antenna, while others watched through their local cable system. Turner, though, wanted more people to see his station.

Turner had no experience in the TV business when

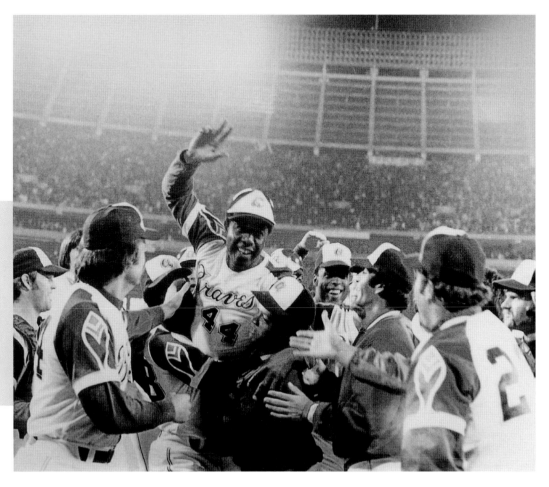

Atlanta Braves player Hank Aaron is congratulated by his teammates after hitting his record-breaking 715th home run on April 8, 1974.

he bought Channel 17 in 1970 and, later that year, another small station in Charlotte, North Carolina. He had briefly owned several radio stations before going into TV, but the Turner family had first made its fortune renting out billboards it owned across the south. Turner took over the family business in 1963 after his father died. At the time, it was one of the largest outdoor advertising companies in the United States. But Turner wanted to do more. He later said, "I thought that television would be more exciting and more interesting."

Ted Turner managed the team for a day when the Braves played Pittsburgh in 1977.

When he decided to buy Channel 17, the station was losing money. People told him the purchase could destroy his whole company. "They said I was crazy," Turner said. "I just love it when people say I can't do something." For Turner, the doubts of others drove him even harder to succeed.

Within 18 months of buying Channel 17, the station made a profit. Buying the rights to the Braves games helped the station grow even more. Turner bought the team itself in 1976 to make sure he could keep televising the games. The next year he bought Atlanta's professional basketball team, the Hawks. Their games were also broadcast on Turner's station.

By the time he bought the Braves, Turner had already started planning to bring their games and other programming to viewers across the country. He was not happy that the three existing TV networks had a great deal of control over what people could watch. Only about one-third of Americans could watch programming from local, independent TV stations. Cable television was available in some parts of the country, but at the beginning of the 1970s, only about 4 million homes paid to receive cable broadcasts. Turner—as a pioneer in the cable industry—was about to help change that.

The year before Turner bought the Braves, the electronics company RCA launched a satellite that could relay TV broadcasts. The satellite was positioned 22,300 miles (35,888 km) above the equator into geosynchronous orbit, meaning it always stayed in the same position relative to a selected spot on the ground. In this case, the satellite remained just west of the United States. The cable network HBO was the first U.S. company to beam its video and audio signal to the satellite. It used an antenna dish about 33 feet (10 m) wide, called an uplink, to send the signals to devices on the satellite called transponders. The transponders then returned the signals to Earth, where cable companies used antenna dishes to receive the signal and then send it to subscribers.

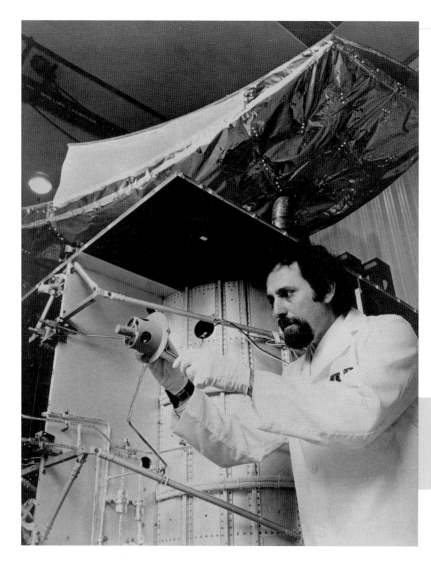

With HBO's success, Turner went into action, paying for access to his own transponders on another RCA satellite. That way, he could make Channel 17 available to cable viewers across the country. The new station went on the air in December 1976. When his SuperStation began, only four cable companies in the United States received its signal. But homes and hotels across the country that had their own satellite dishes could receive the signal directly without going through a cable company. And the signal traveled well beyond the U.S., reaching remote areas of northern Canada and extending south to Central America. Turner met with the owners of cable companies and convinced more of them to carry his station. He also talked to big companies that advertised on the three major networks. Slowly he got more of them to advertise on the SuperStation.

Turner changed the call letters of his station from WTCG to WTBS. The last three letters stood for Turner Broadcasting System. Viewers of WTBS could watch the Braves, the Hawks, and old movies and TV shows. What they did not see was news programming. In the early days of Channel 17, Turner decided that producing his own news was too expensive. But with the launch of the SuperStation, he began to think about a new way to deliver news to the world. He could use a satellite to launch a station that broadcast news—and news alone—24 hours a day. At the time there were no news networks on cable or regular TV that broadcast nationally. Americans could watch only 30 minutes of combined national and international news each night on the Big Three networks or PBS, the public TV network.

Turner first had the idea for an all-news network in 1976. At the time, though, he didn't think enough homes subscribed to cable to make money from a news network. The growing success of WTBS and

HBO helped increase the number of cable subscribers across the U.S. In 1978 Turner was ready to bring his idea to cable. He called Reese Schonfeld, who had a background in TV journalism. Turner explained his idea for the 24-hour news network.

Decades after launching CNN, Reese Schonfeld wrote a book about his time there.

When the two men met, Turner told Schonfeld he wanted to call the new station the Cable News Network. Turner soon sold his Charlotte TV station to finance the creation of CNN. He set June 1, 1980, as the date for the new network's first broadcast.

As president of CNN, Schonfeld hired the people and bought the equipment he needed to carry out Turner's vision of 24-hour news. Even with the money Turner had gotten for the Charlotte station, Schonfeld did not have enough cash to build a news operation like those of the other networks. At times that meant he had to buy used equipment. Meanwhile builders were turning an old private club in Atlanta into CNN's headquarters. The building was large, with several ballrooms and its own basement gym that could be turned into offices and a broadcast studio. The club also had 21 acres of land, meaning CNN had plenty of room for the seven satellite dishes it would use to receive and send television signals.

As the work of turning the club into a studio went on, Turner had to arrange to get transponders on a new RCA satellite. The satellite, though, had not reached geosynchronous orbit after its launch and was useless for CNN. Turner then had to go to court to get RCA to give him access to transponders on another satellite. In February 1980, just three months before CNN was supposed to go on the air, a court ordered RCA to give Turner what he needed.

CNN continued to have problems. In May 1980 the studio was far from finished. The network's weatherman, Flip Spiceland, recalled walking in and seeing floors covered with mud. "One wall had all the windows knocked out, so it was open to the elements." Expensive cameras and other equipment had to be covered with plastic for protection. "And we had no bathrooms. We had portable johns out in the back."

The network was also still installing its own computer system. CNN would be the first news network to have all its reporters and production staff use only computers to do their work. But as the first air date neared, the system still wasn't ready. Computers were still new then. Very few companies had them, and even fewer individuals. Schonfeld's team had to find typewriters and other equipment to share information among the staff. Helping with that work was a team of young college graduates. They lacked professional newsroom experience, but they didn't need to be paid much. The network created what it called CNN College, with the students taking several weeks of classes to learn how CNN would operate.

Saving money was always on Schonfeld's mind. Along with the Atlanta headquarters, CNN had bureaus in New York, Washington, D.C., and other cities. Turner did not want to spend a lot to hire TV news stars, such as Dan Rather, the news anchor at CBS. The people who came to CNN had experience,

"One wall had all the windows knocked out. . . . And we had no bathrooms. We had portable johns out in the back."

but they were not generally well known across the country. One exception was Daniel Schorr, who had worked as a journalist for many years. Some of his reporting for CBS had earned him Emmy awards, the highest honor in the U.S. television industry. Bernie Shaw also was there at the beginning, working out of Washington, D.C.

When Ted Turner debuted CNN, he faced doubts from the established networks.

Finally, despite all the problems in building CNN, the network was ready to go live on June 1, 1980, just as Turner had promised. But he didn't have as many viewers as he wanted. Of almost 5,000 cable systems across the United States, only 172 had agreed to broadcast the new network. Turner had hoped to have 3.5 million cable subscribers able to watch. The actual number on June 1 was less than 2 million. Still, Turner launched CNN with a splashy ceremony. Standing by flags of the state of Georgia, the United States, and the United Nations, he gave a short speech. He promised that CNN would cover international events in depth and "provide information to people when it wasn't available before." He also said CNN would never go off the air. "We will cover the end of the world, live, and that will be our last event." Then a military band played the national anthem, and CNN's first newscast began.

The programming included news segments devoted to business, entertainment, and sports. The major news of the day came on at 8 p.m., though the network could always cut into regular programming for breaking news. CNN also introduced the first national TV call-in show, letting viewers take part in discussing current events. Many of the shows were repeated so people on the West Coast, where it was three hours earlier than on the East Coast, could watch them in the evening.

THE CNN NEWSROOM

Showing viewers the entire newsroom had never been done before CNN started the practice.

When he began creating CNN, Reese Schonfeld wanted to do something that had never been done before in U.S. television news. The major networks showed viewers only the anchors. The reporters and other staff who gathered and prepared the news did not appear on-screen. Schonfeld wanted viewers to see all the activity that happened in the newsroom. He later said, "We want to remove the mystery. And let people feel the excitement!" The idea fit his belief that CNN would always focus on the news rather than the anchors who delivered it.

Schonfeld had seen a TV station in Vancouver, Canada, that put its anchors in the newsroom, but they sat against a wall. CNN viewers would see people working as the anchors talked. Other people in the TV news industry said the idea wouldn't work. The reporters and producers in the newsroom would make too much noise for people to clearly hear the anchors, or the activity would distract them too much. But Schonfeld refused to change his vision, and other TV networks later copied this "open newsroom" concept. Years later Turner praised Schonfeld for the idea, which had helped CNN stand out from the other TV networks. Turner said, "We wanted to look immediate, up-to-the minute, that things are happening at our place."

Some of the first shows did not go smoothly. At one point, viewers saw a janitor at work in the CNN studio. Rival networks insulted CNN by taking the network's three initials and calling it "chicken noodle news." The rival networks were suggesting that CNN could not be taken seriously as a source of news. But at least one TV critic saw the way CNN would change how people got their news. Arthur Unger of the *Christian Science Monitor* described how one late-night program gave him information hours before he saw it in his daily newspaper. Unger wrote, "I was able to realize that something extraordinary was going on." In the days before the internet, CNN was the national source for news, any time of day. This was revolutionary.

But CNN faced other challenges. Turner had to go to court to get permission for his reporters to receive news reports from what was called the presidential pool. The major broadcast networks did not always send their own cameras to cover Ronald Reagan, who became president in 1981. Instead, a different network went every day and then shared the video with the other two—but they refused to share with CNN. Winning the legal challenge gave CNN access to the pool reports.

The network also struggled to get more viewers, though it did make deals with networks in other countries. CNN broadcast its reports to those

"I was able to realize that something extraordinary was going on."

countries, and in return it had access to reports from foreign networks. So CNN became the first global news network. CNN also made deals with local TV stations across the United States. They provided video footage of news events in their regions. In exchange they got CNN's coverage of events that the major networks might not have.

On January 1, 1982, CNN began a second network, CNN2, that offered "headline" news—short reports on the most important events, repeated throughout the day. Turner launched the new CNN2 network after he learned that ABC was preparing a similar headline-news network that would rely on satellites. ABC had more money, so Turner wanted to get his new network on the air first, and he did.

Peter Arnett (left) and Bernard Shaw would later win awards for their early work at CNN.

Through the 1980s other big media companies considered competing against CNN. But Turner had attracted many loyal viewers. At the beginning of 1983, the number of cable subscribers who could watch CNN had jumped to more than 10 million.

Through the 1980s that number continued to grow, and the number of people who watched CNN usually rose when an important news story happened. These included the explosion of the space shuttle *Challenger* in 1986 and protests by Chinese students against their government in 1989. CNN also showed that it was becoming as important as the Big Three networks when Shaw was chosen to moderate a presidential debate in 1988. That year CNN made $89 million, and it and CNN2 were soon worth more than $1 billion. At the same time, the broadcast network news sometimes lost money.

For its 10th anniversary, CNN hired actor James Earl Jones to record a simple message: "This is CNN." The audio clip became famous thanks to Jones's familiar, deep voice. He had also done the voice for Darth Vader in the *Star Wars* movies. Soon after that anniversary, CNN would become famous for much more than that clip. The network's importance as a source of news only grew after Saddam Hussein decided to invade Kuwait.

Chapter Three

PRAISE AND CHALLENGES

"... if you ask, are some stories worth the risk of dying for, my answer is yes."

After the initial U.S.–led attack on Baghdad in the early hours of January 17, 1991, more waves of planes bombed the city. Shaw told the television audience watching CNN that he was too afraid to go sleep. "I don't want to miss anything . . . and I don't like to go to sleep where bombs are falling." But that evening Iraqi officials forced the CNN team to shut down its broadcast. The crew went to the bomb shelter in the hotel basement.

Most of the CNN team left Baghdad the next day, and Iraq soon told all reporters from Allied countries to leave. The only reporter allowed to stay was CNN's Peter Arnett—with a few members of his team. He later said that he guessed the Iraqis let CNN remain because of its global presence. Also, the Iraqis told him they thought CNN's coverage since the August 1990 invasion of Kuwait had been fair. Arnett chose to stay, he said, because "reporting is what I do for a living . . . if you ask, are some stories worth the risk of dying for, my answer is yes."

A bomb knocked out the four-wire, so Arnett took out a satellite phone CNN had bought. The phone's equipment was about the size of a large suitcase, with its own uplink satellite dish. Iraqi officials said he could use it only while they were present. Though

the Americans did not target the Al-Rashid Hotel, where he was staying, Arnett did see the effects of the war firsthand. One day Iraqi forces shot down a U.S. cruise missile before it reached its target. The explosion started a fire in the hotel and destroyed a part of the lobby.

THE LYING JOURNALIST?

During the Gulf War, the U.S. military bombed this factory, which it said produced chemical weapons. Arnett reported that it created infant formula. Arnett's claim received backing after the war.

While CNN won many positive reviews of its coverage of the Gulf War, not all Americans were pleased with Peter Arnett's reporting. Born in New Zealand, Arnett had become a U.S. citizen just before the war. Earlier in his career, he had covered the Vietnam War for the Associated Press and won a Pulitzer Prize, the highest honor in U.S. journalism. Arnett started working for CNN in 1981. During the Gulf War, he had to write out his reports and let Iraqi officials review them before he went on the air. He managed to bypass the censors somewhat when he did question-and-answer sessions with CNN's anchors in Atlanta. But in the U.S., some people criticized Arnett for seeming to present Iraqi propaganda.

At one point a spokesman for President George H.W. Bush called him a liar. The U.S. military claimed that its bombs were not killing Iraqi civilians. Some of Arnett's reports said otherwise. He reported from a bombed factory that he said was used to make infant formula. U.S officials claimed it was actually producing chemical weapons. The people who opposed Arnett said he was either lying or being tricked by the Iraqis. In the U.S., CNN received hundreds of letters every day expressing anger over Arnett's reporting. Some companies stopped advertising on the network. To try to soften some of the criticism, CNN had military analyst Major General Perry Smith address Arnett's reporting. He defended the accuracy of the U.S. bombs and the efforts to avoid civilian casualties. As far as what was produced in the factory, a U.S. government document released after the war seemed to support Arnett's claim and dispute the government's.

Another time, while in his room, Arnett saw a U.S. missile roar past his window on its way to a nearby target. And, one day, a blast in the hotel destroyed his portable typewriter, so Arnett had to write out all of his reports by hand. The Iraqis insisted on approving them before they aired.

The Iraqi government also would not allow Arnett to leave the hotel on his own to see the effects of the bombing. A government official would always go with him. During his stay, Arnett walked around the city with thousands of dollars in cash stuffed into his jacket. He needed cash because, in a country that was mostly without power after the bombings, that was the only way to pay for goods and services.

Back in the United States, CNN, like the Big Three networks, hired former military officers to analyze the events in Iraq. CNN, though, had its experts available almost all day and night, and they provided more analysis than the other networks did. CNN also showed viewers the daily reports from U.S. military commanders in the Middle East. Americans fascinated by the events in Iraq could tune in to CNN at any time for the latest news.

Some of the CNN staff became well known, thanks to the network's 24-hour coverage. Wolf Blitzer was often on the air, reporting from the Pentagon. That building is the headquarters of the U.S. military. After the war Blitzer said some people

"I say: 'Look, I didn't go to Saudi Arabia, Iraq, or Kuwait. I was standing in front of a map at the Pentagon.'"

commented on his bravery. "I say: 'Look, I didn't go to Saudi Arabia, Iraq, or Kuwait. I was standing in front of a map at the Pentagon.'" Starting in late February, Iraq let more journalists into the country, and Christiane Amanpour joined Arnett as a CNN reporter. She had grown up in both Iran and England and had started at CNN in 1983. Amanpour won praise for the tough questions she asked the Iraqi officials. By then CNN and other networks had broadcast some video footage from Baghdad and cities that Iraq targeted with its missiles. Americans had seen video footage during earlier wars, especially Vietnam. But with the Gulf War, satellites provided the images live or very soon after they were recorded. And the coverage from CNN and other international news agencies let the whole world watch the war as it unfolded.

After bombing Iraqi targets, the U.S.–led forces attacked on the ground. They quickly freed Kuwait from Iraqi control and then went into Iraq itself. The fighting ended on February 28. According to at least one poll, U.S. viewers thought CNN had provided

Christiane Amanpour traveled all over the world for CNN, including Iran.

the best coverage of the war. CNN's slogan was "the most trusted name in news," and more people were starting to agree. The *Los Angeles Times* wrote on March 1 that CNN was one of the "winners" in the war. "If there was a doubt that CNN was not the news network of record—and the most influential news presence on the globe—it was removed by the Gulf conflict." At the end of 1991 *Time* magazine named Ted Turner its "Man of the Year," praising CNN's coverage of events around the world, including the Gulf War. The magazine wrote that Turner had changed the news "from something that has happened to something that is happening at the very moment you are hearing of it."

In 1991 Ted Turner was named "Man of the Year" by *Time* magazine for creating a network that reported the news as it happened.

CNN continued to grow during the 1990s. By 1996 it was available in 68 million homes across the U.S. The money the network made from ads rose too, doubling between 1990 and 1995. The Big Three networks also felt pressure from their owners to make money from news broadcasts. That had not been true before the rise of CNN, when the networks could afford to lose money on their news broadcasts. They knew their entertainment programming would make plenty of money. But with the growth of cable TV, viewers had many more choices of what to watch. That meant the networks made less money from their programming.

Still, at the end of the 1990s, millions more people continued to watch network nightly news than watched cable news. And the networks were offering more news programming than they had before, usually hour-long shows that featured two or three stories. These "magazine" shows included *48 Hours* on CBS and *Dateline NBC*. They often aired during prime time—between 8 p.m. and 11 p.m.

The rise of CNN saw changes at some local TV affiliates. In larger cities, many increased the amount of news they showed each day—some offered up to six hours of news. The networks had stuck with their 30-minute evening news broadcasts, not counting the magazine programming. Those nightly newscasts also changed over time. The networks covered fewer

"If there was a doubt that CNN was not the news network of record . . . it was removed by the Gulf conflict."

international events and offered less headline news to show more live interviews or reports on such topics as health and safety and weather. The networks realized more viewers were turning to cable for headlines and on-the-spot reporting. The networks also set up internet sites to provide people with 24-hour news, even if it wasn't on their televisions.

One network made a direct challenge to CNN by creating a 24-hour cable station that carried business news. NBC had launched CNBC in 1989, but like CNN in its early days, it struggled to get onto cable systems. CNBC also targeted a very specific audience—business leaders and investors. With the rise of CNN, NBC wanted a general news network. It partnered with software maker Microsoft to launch MSNBC in 1996.

That same year, CNN had gone through a big change on its business side. Turner agreed to sell all his television networks to Time Warner. That huge media company owned HBO, cable systems, magazines, book publishers, and a movie studio. Turner owned just over 10 percent of the new company, though he remained in control of Turner Broadcasting, which included CNN.

The Time Warner deal came after another media multimillionaire decided to enter the business of cable news. Australian-born Rupert Murdoch owned newspapers, a film studio, and the Fox Broadcasting

Rupert Murdoch went to battle with Ted Turner when he created the Fox News network.

Company, a fourth TV network he had launched in 1986. Now Murdoch was building Fox News. Murdoch and Turner did not like each other. Murdoch's newspaper, the *New York Post*, sometimes insulted Turner, suggesting he was crazy. Turner, in one interview, called Murdoch a "megalomaniac." Turner went on, "I don't think there's a spark of human decency in him—except he likes his family." The battle of the cable news networks was about to begin.

THE CNN EFFECT

The plight of starving people in Somalia, as shown on CNN, may have led to relief efforts.

During the 1990s some media experts began to discuss what they called "the CNN effect." By some accounts, this supposed power of CNN and other news media to shape public opinion began in 1992. That year, CNN broadcast images showing the effects of a terrible famine in the African country of Somalia. About 250,000 people died of starvation. President George H.W. Bush sent food to Somalia and then sent troops to help protect workers giving out the food. Some people credited CNN's coverage with stirring the president to act, as more Americans spoke out against the suffering in Somalia. The influence of CNN and other cable news networks was reflected in other ways. Some world leaders said they first learned about trouble around the world through the cable networks. These leaders sometimes made comments to CNN that they wanted other leaders to hear, knowing they also watched the cable news.

In recent years, scholars have debated how strong the CNN effect really is. Governments still largely make their decisions based on what is in their country's best interest and do not respond to what is shown on TV. In 2018 journalist Uri Friedman said the CNN effect seemed to have no effect on the ongoing Syrian civil war. People around the world saw news reports on the killing of civilians, but other governments and the United Nations did not take strong steps to try to stop it. On the other hand, President Donald Trump said he decided to carry out one attack on Syria after seeing photos on TV of children killed there. That seemed to be one sign of the CNN effect at work.

Chapter Four

REPORTING THE NEWS IN A NEW CENTURY

With Fox News on the air, CNN faced competition from two 24-hour cable news networks. Its ratings had slipped, and Fox had specifically targeted a new audience: Americans who thought CNN and other news networks were too liberal in their views. Fox said its coverage was "fair and balanced," but its leaders promoted a conservative viewpoint. An article in the *Columbia Journalism Review* said that some reporters complained about the pressure they faced from Fox officials. They wanted reporters to "cook the facts" to present a certain view of the news.

CNN officials thought they could use their connection with Time Warner's magazines to present in-depth stories that no other network carried. One of the first such stories aired in 1998, a report called "Valley of Death," which was part of a new program done with *Time* magazine. Peter Arnett was the lead reporter. "Valley of Death" claimed that the U.S. government had used poison gas during the Vietnam War to kill U.S. soldiers who had left their posts and fled to the Asian nation of Laos. The operation had the code name Tailwind. Many network officials approved the reporting done for the show. Right before it aired, CNN president Tom Johnson learned that military officials claimed the story was not true.

The government lied about the effects of Agent Orange during the Vietnam War. The anger about that lie might have been one reason reporters believed the false report about poison gas.

But CNN went ahead with the broadcast.

When people learned that CNN's story was, in fact, false, some attacked the network for showing the U.S. military in a bad light. All news media sometimes get a story wrong, but with the

Tailwind story, CNN ignored some of the rules of good journalism. For one, CNN seemed to rely on evidence that did not definitely show that the government was trying to kill U.S. soldiers. They also seemed to ignore some evidence that did not support its story.

CNN investigated its own reporting and admitted it had made a mistake in airing the program. The network fired several people connected to the story, and Peter Arnett soon left CNN. Johnson went on TV to apologize. He said CNN had not followed its usual standards for presenting accurate news. He promised, "We are taking vigorous steps . . . to assure that mistakes of this type do not occur in the future." Turner said handling the reaction to the Tailwind story was "the most horrible nightmare I've ever lived through."

Tom Johnson apologized on TV for his decision to run the Tailwind story.

The incident seemed to boost the Fox News claim that CNN could not be trusted to present the news accurately. Meanwhile MSNBC was trying to make its name by being more liberal than CNN. For a time, it seemed to work. Among the three all-news networks, it was second after CNN in the ratings. Fox began to pick up viewers in early 1999, when President Bill Clinton faced impeachment and its news commentators strongly attacked Clinton. The next year, as George W. Bush ran against Vice President Al Gore for president, even more viewers turned to Fox News. It passed MSNBC in the ratings. Two years later, Fox topped CNN to become the most-watched news network.

Fox News was friendly to politicians who shared its conservative views, including Vice President Dick Cheney (left).

By then CNN had gone through more business changes. In 2000 Time Warner merged with AOL, which was a leading internet service with about 25 million subscribers. At the time it was the largest deal ever that combined two existing companies into one. CNN was just one small part of the company, and some staff disliked the new arrangement. Frank Sesno was in charge of CNN's Washington, D.C., bureau at that time. He thought AOL was more focused on making money than on delivering good news. Sesno later said, "One of the first things I did at the bureau was lay off 10 percent of the staff. That's one of the reasons I left CNN . . ." Sesno did not want to play a role in weakening the network.

The deal also meant that Ted Turner had no direct control over the network he had created. In the past Turner had told CNN to do news specials on certain topics he cared about, and it happened—even if the shows lost money. After the AOL deal, CNN refused to spend the money that Turner wanted to make a documentary on the spread of nuclear weapons. With the new company, Johnson said, "there is much less enthusiasm for high-cost, low audience long-form documentaries that were near and dear to Ted's heart."

With the AOL deal, CNN faced a problem that was beginning to spread throughout all forms of journalism. It was harder for media companies to

Top executives held a press conference to announce the acquisition of Time Warner by AOL.

make money presenting the news, especially with the growth of the internet. The introduction of web browsers that were easy to use let millions of people access content on the internet. Newspapers and other news sources published their content on the web, and fewer people watched network and cable TV news. Later, the spread of social media such as Facebook and Twitter led even more people to get much or all of their news online. CNN, like other TV networks, had its own website, and at times it reported news there that was not shown on TV. CNN and other outlets had to collect and report the news 24 hours

CNN Exclusive

a day, seven days a week. The pressure to provide the news quickly and constantly only increased with such important stories as the terrorist attacks on the United States on September 11, 2001.

Anyone could put up an internet site, call it news, and present a mixture of facts and lies. And few websites paid money to hire people to collect the news, as CNN and major newspapers did. Often those sites simply repeated stories already aired on CNN or other networks. Ratings for the cable news networks were in decline. CNN in particular seemed hurt by the changes in how people got their news. In 2013 its ratings during the prime-time hours trailed both Fox and MSNBC. Viewers seemed to prefer the clear political views presented on those two networks or the instant access they got through the internet. CNN, meanwhile, tried to be objective in reporting all news fairly and offering a range of political opinions. And some media experts thought the network was still too serious compared to the other networks.

In 2013 Time Warner hired Jeff Zucker to win back viewers. Zucker had once run all of NBC. Some of his first moves included firing commentators who had been on CNN for years and hiring new reporters and commentators. One of them was Jake Tapper, who had begun his career as a congressional press secretary before becoming a prizewinning print journalist based in Washington, D.C. He soon joined Anderson Cooper as one of the best-known CNN reporters and anchors. Cooper had his own show, which aired nightly, and he won praise for his coverage of Hurricane Katrina in 2005.

Zucker also shifted news coverage from airing many stories a day to providing more detail on fewer stories. He said that CNN was founded on the idea that in 22 minutes, it could cover all the important news events of the day. "But that's not the way people consume news and information any more. So on television we are going to go much deeper on the one,

two, or three stories of real significance or interest that day." Zucker also added programming that had little to do with news—such as a regular program about food and travel.

Zucker also wanted to boost CNN's existing presence online and hired several dozen people to help with that effort. He said in 2013, "We are not going to care what screen you are watching CNN on" and reaching viewers through their mobile phones "is probably the most important part of our future." In August 2014 the network reported more than 120 million visits to its website. That number was 32 percent higher than the year before.

In 2016 CNN got a boost in ratings thanks to the presidential election. Interest was high across the country, since Democrat Hillary Rodham Clinton was trying to become the first woman president in the U.S. On the Republican side, billionaire Donald Trump won attention as he frequently insulted the other Republicans running during the primaries. He came across as someone who said what he thought. CNN and other news networks often aired broadcasts of Trump's rallies, and he also appeared on the many debates carried on the networks. CNN invited Trump onto its news shows. The candidate also phoned in to some of the network's shows.

Thanks in part to its coverage of the election, CNN made almost $1 billion in 2016, its most ever for one year at that time. But as the campaign went on, its relationship with Trump grew tense. He complained to Zucker that Jake Tapper asked too many tough questions. Trump also hated the fact that CNN would declare that some of his statements were untrue while he was still talking. Trump said he would stop doing interviews with CNN.

After Trump won the presidency, he continued to feud with CNN. At his first meeting with reporters in January 2017, Trump refused to call on a CNN reporter. Trump said. "Not you. Your organization is terrible. . . . You are fake news." As the year went on, he increasingly said that CNN, along with

DANA BASH AND U.S. POLITICS

Dana Bash attained star status during the 2016 presidential election.

During recent U.S. presidential elections, Dana Bash has been a familiar face to CNN viewers. Bash started her career at CNN in 1993, working behind the camera. Her first job was in the network's tape library at its Washington, D.C., bureau. She soon worked her way up to become a producer at the bureau. Bash helped choose stories related to Congress, the president, and important political issues. She began reporting on presidential campaigns during 2000, and with each election after, Bash played a larger role in CNN's coverage of the races. By 2016 Bash was CNN's top Washington correspondent. During the election that year, she interviewed many of the candidates and asked questions at the debates that aired on CNN. Those debates took place during the primaries, the elections held in each state to choose a party's candidate. In an interview after the election, Bash noted the increasing importance of social media, especially Twitter, in helping candidates reach a large audience. She also talked about the importance of the internet for CNN. "Whenever I complete a TV segment, the very first thing I do is make sure it's online, because that's how most people will see it. And you can continue to keep it alive. Thankfully CNN is on top of it."

President Trump often yells "fake news" at reporters during press conferences.

other media outlets, reported "fake news." To some reporters, what Trump called fake—meaning not true—was any news that he did not like.

A media organization called FactCheck.org looked at Trump's claims about specific stories he called fake. It reported in January 2018, "There are times . . . when he has labeled accurate news reporting as 'fake news' or spread false information himself, while at the same time accusing the media of being 'fake' or 'dishonest.'" The same report noted that more Americans believed major news outlets reported "fake news" than had the year before.

As Trump's attacks on the media continued, CNN's Chris Cillizza made this point in 2018. "To Trump . . . negative news coverage is fake news. Fake news is negative news coverage. This is, of course, not true . . . media coverage that he feels is not sufficiently favorable to him—is not, by definition, fake. Fake news is made-up news. It's not based in traditional reporting values like facts and sourcing. It's not 'news' at all."

Both the FactCheck.org report and Cillizza's comments stressed this point: The media do make mistakes in reporting the news. But when they learn of those mistakes, the best media companies admit it, as CNN did with its Tailwind reporting in 1998. In some cases, the media will fire the people responsible for the mistakes. But making mistakes is not the same thing as reporting false information.

For President Trump, however, CNN remained the top target for his attacks on "fake news." At a press conference in November 2018, he became angry with CNN's Jim Acosta when the reporter tried to ask another question after the president had already answered one. Trump called Acosta a "rude, terrible person. You shouldn't be working for CNN." Later the Trump administration said it would no longer let Acosta report from the White House.

CNN responded by suing Trump and several of his staff members. The network claimed, in part,

> "To Trump . . . negative news coverage is fake news. Fake news is negative news coverage. This is, of course not true . . ."

that keeping Acosta out of the White House violated his and CNN's constitutional rights. CNN and other reporters said the president had no legal power to choose which journalists could or couldn't report on his actions. The U.S. Department of Justice argued in court that Trump did have that right. Trump's actions worried other journalists, including former White House correspondent Sam Donaldson. In a statement supporting Acosta and CNN, he said, "If denying access to a reporter an organization has chosen to represent it—in effect asserting the president's right to take that choice away from a news organization and make it himself—is permitted, then the press is not free." Nearly two weeks later, the White House restored Acosta's credentials but instituted new rules for journalists. These included the White House deciding when a follow-up question could be asked.

CNN is committed to keeping the media free for all journalists. And its reporters and producers continue to try to present the most accurate news they can. The network, on its commentary shows, tries to offer a range of opinions. It faces challenges from the competition on cable TV and the internet. But no one doubts the way CNN changed how the media report the news, providing information 24 hours every day. CNN will continue to play an important role in providing the world with news—just as Ted Turner had hoped decades before.

Timeline

1963

Ted Turner takes over his father's billboard business.

1970

Turner buys Channel 17 in Atlanta and begins expanding its broadcast range.

1978

Turner meets with TV journalist Reese Schonfeld to begin the creation of Cable News Network (CNN).

1980

CNN goes on the air on June 1.

1973

Turner begins airing the Atlanta Braves baseball team on his station.

1976

Turner begins broadcasting Channel 17 across the country using a satellite, creating what he called a SuperStation.

1982

CNN2, later called CNN Headline News, goes on the air.

1988

CNN anchor Bernie Shaw is chosen to moderate a presidential debate.

Timeline

1991

CNN wins praise for its coverage of the Gulf War in Iraq.

1996

CNN is available in 68 million homes across the United States. NBC and Microsoft start MSNBC to compete with CNN. Rupert Murdoch starts the Fox News network to compete with CNN. Turner sells his TV networks to Time Warner.

2002

Fox News beats CNN in the ratings for the first time.

2013

Jeff Zucker takes over CNN and tries to improve its falling ratings as it faces competition from the internet and social media.

1998

CNN makes false claims about the U.S. military in its Tailwind report; the network makes a public apology.

2000

Time Warner merges with AOL. Turner no longer has direct control over CNN.

2017

President Donald Trump accuses CNN and other major news companies of delivering "fake news." Many journalists believe that the president simply dislikes any facts that show him in a negative light.

Glossary

affiliates—local television stations that carry the shows broadcast by a particular national network

Allied—when capitalized, a reference to the United States and the countries helping it fight a common enemy

bureau—office for gathering news that is located away from a news organization's main headquarters

conservative—in politics, tending to believe that people should have great amounts of individual freedom, especially in business, and that the government should have limited powers

documentary—film that presents facts about current or historical events, offering more detail than a typical news broadcast

geosynchronous—always staying in the same position relative to a selected spot on the ground

impeachment—the process of charging an elected official with a serious crime; it can result in removal from office

liberal—in politics, tending to believe that the government, especially the national government, should play an active role in shaping the economy and defending the rights of groups that historically have not had their rights protected

producer—the person who helps choose and put together a television news story

propaganda—information, often false or incomplete, spread by a government to influence others' actions and beliefs

subscriber—person who pays a regular fee, usually monthly or yearly, to receive a certain product or service

Additional Resources

Further Reading

Eboch, M.M. *A History of Television*. Minneapolis: Essential Library, 2015.

Gilbert, Sara. *The Story of CNN*. Mankato, MN: Creative Education, 2013.

Streissguth, Thomas. *The Persian Gulf War*. San Diego: ReferencePoint Press, 2018.

Vance, Lucian. *Fake News and Media Bias*. New York: Lucent Press, 2018.

Internet Sites

History of Cable
https://www.calcable.org/larn/history-of-cable/

MSNBC
http://www.msnbc.com

Ted Turner
https://www.biography.com/people/ted-turner-9512255

Critical Thinking Questions

A few decades ago, people read daily newspapers and watched the news on TV. How do you think the availability of 24/7 news has changed our expectations about receiving information?

CNN has tried to position itself as the objective news network. In recent years, cable news networks that are openly political have surpassed CNN in the ratings. Why do you think this has happened?

Explain why the term "fake news" is being widely used when it refers to objective news with which the subject of the news disagrees.

Source Notes

p. 7, "You spend whatever you think it takes, pal…" Ken Auletta. *Media Man: Ted Turner's Improbable Empire.* New York: Atlas Books, 2004, p. 53.

p. 9, "I will take on myself…" Ibid., p. 54.

p. 9, "We'd wake up in the morning feeling brave…" Ingrid Formanek, "Operation Desert Storm: 25 Years On," CNN.com, January 19, 2016, https://www.cnn.com/2016/01/19/middleeast/operation-desert-storm-25-years-later/index.html

p. 10, "and I leave Baghdad…" Howard Kurtz, "Bernard Shaw, Under Siege," *Washington Post*, January 22, 1991, https://www.washingtonpost.com/archive/lifestyle/1991/01/22/bernard-shaw-under-siege/339c65c3-ff26-41fa-9ffe-8b274aae2fb0/?utm_term=.6df970b9b18a.

p. 10, "The Iraqis really thought…" "Operation Desert Storm: 25 Years On."

p. 11, "Something is happening outside…" Robert Wiener, *Live from Baghdad: Gathering News at Ground Zero.* New York: Doubleday, 1992, p. 259.

p. 12, "We hear the sound…" David Shedden, "Today in Media History: The Gulf War's 1991 Operation Desert Storm," Poynter.org, January 16, 2015, https://www.poynter.org/news/today-media-history-gulf-wars-1991-operation-desert-storm

p. 14, "Now there's a huge fire that we've just seen…" Peter Arnett. *Live from the Battlefield: From Vietnam to Baghdad 35 Years in the World's War Zones.* New York: Simon & Schuster, 1994, p. 367.

p. 14, "John, we do still hear you." Ibid.

p. 17, "I thought that television would be…" *Media Man*, p. 30.

p. 18, "They said I was crazy…" Hank Whittemore. *CNN: The Inside Story.* Boston: Little, Brown and Company, 1990, p. 14.

p. 24, "One wall had all the windows… " *Inside Story*, p. 123.

p. 26, "Provide information…" Ibid., p. 143.

p. 26, "We will cover the end of the world…" Thor Benson, "Alleged CNN 'Doomsday' Video for the End of the World from the 1980s Released," UPI.com, January 5, 2015, https://www.upi.com/Odd_News/2015/01/05/Alleged-CNN-doomsday-video-for-the-end-of-the-world-from-the-1980s-released/2671420505012/

p. 27, "We want to remove the mystery…" Ibid., p. 57.

p. 27, "We wanted to look immediate…" "This Is CNN's 30th Anniversary," Emmys.com, http://m.emmys.com/news/interviews-project-news/cnns-30th-anniversary

p. 28, "I was able to realize that…" Reese Schonfeld. *Me and Ted Against the World: The Unathorized Story of the Founding of CNN.* New York: Cliff Street, 2001, p. 191.

p. 31, "I don't want to miss anything…" *Live from Baghdad*, p. 266.

p. 31, "reporting is what I do…" Perry M. Smith, *How CNN Fought the War: A View from the Inside.* New York: Birch Lane Press, 1991, p. 37.

p. 35, "I say: 'Look, I didn't go to Saudi Arabia, Iraq or Kuwait…" Eric Schmitt, "Five Years Later, The Gulf War Story Is Still Being Told," *New York Times*, May 12, 1996, https://www.nytimes.com/1996/05/12/arts/television-five-years-later-the-gulf-war-story-is-still-being-told.html

p. 37, "If there was a doubt that CNN was not…" Howard Rosenberg, "TV and the Gulf War: Who Won, Who Lost in Media Coverage of Conflict," *Los Angeles Times*, March 1, 1991, http://articles.latimes.com/1991-03-01/news/mn-2269_1_gulf-war

p. 37, "from something that has happened…" "Ted Turner Named Time's 'Man of the Year.'" UPI.com, December 28, 1991, https://www.upi.com/Archives/1991/12/28/Ted-Turner-named-Times-Man-of-the-Year/6522693896400/

p. 40, "I don't think there's a spark of human decency…" *Media Man*, p. 81.

p. 42, "cook the facts…" Scott Collins. *Crazy Like a Fox: The Inside Story of How Fox News Beat CNN.* New York: Portfolio, 2004, p. 150.

p. 44, "The most horrible nightmare…" *Crazy Like a Fox*, p. 108.

p. 46, "One of the first things I did at the bureau…" Lloyd Grove. "The Perils of an AT&T-Time Warner Merger," *Daily Beast*, October 26, 2016, https://www.thedailybeast.com/the-perils-of-an-atandt-time-warner-merger

p. 46, "There is much less enthusiasm…" *Media Man*, p. 109.

p. 49, "But that's not the way people consume news…" Jasper Jackson, "CNN's Jeff Zucker: 'People Want Someone to Blame for Donald Trump's Rise,'" *The Guardian*, April 24, 2016, https://www.theguardian.com/media/2016/apr/24/cnn-jeff-zucker-donald-trump-vice

p. 50, "We are not going to care what screen…" Miguel Helft, "CNN's Jeff Zucker: Digital Is Our Future," *Forbes*, July 23, 2013, http://fortune.com/2013/07/23/cnns-jeff-zucker-digital-is-our-future/

p. 51, "Not you…" "Trump to CNN Reporter: You Are Fake News," CBNC, January 11, 2017, https://www.cnbc.com/video/2017/01/11/trump-to-cnn-reporter-you-are-fake-news.html

p. 52, "Whenever I complete a TV segment …" Samantha Holender and Elisabeth Lobel, "An Interview With Dana Bash: GW Alum and Chief Political Correspondent for CNN," Her Campus at George Washington, December 5, 2016, George Washington University, https://www.hercampus.com/school/gwu/interview-dana-bash-gw-alum-and-chief-political-correspondent-cnn

p. 53, "There are times…" Eugene Kiely, "Trump's Phony 'Fake News' Claims," FactCheck.org, January 16, 2018, Annenberg Public Policy Center, https://www.factcheck.org/2018/01/trumps-phony-fake-news

p. 54, "To Trump…" Chris Cillizza, "Donald Trump Just Accidentally Revealed Something Very Important About His 'Fake News' Attacks," CNN.com, May 9, 2018, https://www.cnn.com/2018/05/09/politics/donald-trump-media-tweet/index.html

p. 54, "A rude, terrible person…" Kyle Swenson, "How CNN's Jim Acosta Became the Reporter Trump Loves to Hate," *Washington Post*, November 8, 2018, https://www.washingtonpost.com/nation/2018/11/08/how-cnns-jim-acosta-became-reporter-trump-loves-hate/?utm_term=.4b0a41f9ea5711/8

p. 55, "If denying access to a reporter…" Brian Stelter and David Shortell, "Trump Argues in Court Filing That He Can Limit Journalists' Access to White House," Washington Post, November 14, 2018, https://www.cnn.com/2018/11/14/media/trump-response-cnn-lawsuit/index.html

All internet sites were accessed and available as of November 15, 2018.

Select Bibliography

Adalian, Josef. "Has Jeff Zucker Made CNN Better?" *New York*, January 9, 2014. http://nymag.com/daily/intelligencer/2014/01/has-jeff-zucker-made-cnn-better.html Accessed on May 8, 2018.

Arnett, Peter. *Live from the Battlefield: From Vietnam to Baghdad 35 Years in the World's War Zones*. New York: Simon & Schuster, 1994.

Auletta, Ken. *Media Man: Ted Turner's Improbable Empire*. New York: Atlas Books, 2004.

Benson, Thor. "Alleged CNN 'Doomsday' Video for the End of the World from the 1980s Released." UPI.com, January 5, 2015, https://www.upi.com/Odd_News/2015/01/05/Alleged-CNN-doomsday-video-for-the-end-of-the-world-from-the-1980s-released/2671420505012/ Accessed on May 3, 2018.

"Bernard Shaw: A Look Back on the 10th Anniversary of the Gulf War." CNN.com, January 16, 2001. http://www.cnn.com/chat/transcripts/2001/01/16/shaw/ Accessed on April 10, 2018.

Capachi, Casey. "Wolf Blitzer Reflects on Covering the Gulf War 25 Years Ago." CNN.com, March 1, 2016. https://www.cnn.com/2016/03/01/politics/wolf-blitzer-gulf-war-iraq-kuwait-cnn/index.html Accessed on April 30, 2018.

Cillizza, Chris. "Donald Trump Just Accidentally Revealed Something Very Important About His 'Fake News' Attacks." CNN.com, May 9, 2018. https://www.cnn.com/2018/05/09/politics/donald-trump-media-tweet/index.html Accessed on May 10, 2018.

"CNN Reigns in Desert Storm," *Variety*, January 20, 1991. http://variety.com/1991/more/news/cnn-reigns-in-desert-storm-99128411/ Accessed on April 10, 2018.

"CNN Retracts Tailwind Coverage." CNN.com, July 2, 1998. http://www.cnn.com/US/9807/02/tailwind.johnson/ Accessed on April 30, 2018.

Collins, Scott. *Crazy Like a Fox: The Inside Story of How Fox News Beat CNN*. New York: Portfolio, 2004.

Formanek, Ingrid. "Operation Desert Storm: 25 Years On." CNN.com, January 19, 2016. https://www.cnn.com/2016/01/19/middleeast/operation-desert-storm-25-years-later/index.html Accessed on March 14, 2018.

Friedman, Uri. "The 'CNN Effect' Dies in Syria." *The Atlantic*, March 1, 2018. https://www.theatlantic.com/international/archive/2018/03/cnn-effect-syria/554387/ Accessed on May 5, 2018.

Gunther, Marc. "The Transformation of Network News." NiemanReports, June 15, 1999. Nieman Foundation, http://niemanreports.org/articles/the-transformation-of-network-news/ Accessed on May 2, 2018.

Holender, Samantha, and Elisabeth Lobel. "An Interview With Dana Bash: GW Alum and Chief Political Correspondent for CNN." Her Campus at George Washington, December 5, 2016. George Washington University, https://www.hercampus.com/school/gwu/interview-dana-bash-gw-alum-and-chief-political-correspondent-cnn Accessed on May 8, 2018.

Jackson, Jasper. "CNN's Jeff Zucker: 'People Want Someone to Blame for Donald Trump's Rise.'" *The Guardian*, April 24, 2016. https://www.theguardian.com/media/2016/apr/24/cnn-jeff-zucker-donald-trump-vice Accessed on May 5, 2018.

Kiely, Eugene. "Trump's Phony 'Fake News' Claims." FactCheck.org, January 16, 2018. Annenberg Public Policy Center, https://www.factcheck.org/2018/01/trumps-phony-fake-news-claims/ Accessed on May 10, 2018.

Kurtz, Howard. "Bernard Shaw, Under Siege." *Washington Post*, January 22, 1991. https://www.washingtonpost.com/archive/lifestyle/1991/01/22/bernard-shaw-under-siege/339c65c3-ff26-41fa-9ffe-8b274aae2fb0/?utm_term=.6df970b9b18a Accessed on April 1, 2018.

Mahler, Jonathan. "CNN Had a Problem. Donald Trump Solved It." *New York Times Magazine*, April 4, 2017. https://www.nytimes.com/2017/04/04/magazine/cnn-had-a-problem-donald-trump-solved-it.html Accessed on March 12, 2018.

McDougal, Dennis. "How CNN Won Battle for a Phone Line." *Los Angeles Times*, January 25, 1991. http://articles.latimes.com/1991-01-25/entertainment/ca-710_1_all-news-network Accessed on April 12, 2018.

Miller, Mark Crispin. "A Lesson In U.S. Propaganda." AlterNet, January 2, 2003. https://www.alternet.org/story/14877/a_lesson_in_u.s._propaganda Accessed on April 30, 2018.

Pike, Sidney. *We Changed the World: Memoirs of a CNN Satellite Pioneer*. St. Paul, MN: Paragon House, 2005.

Rosenberg, Howard. "TV and the Gulf War: Who Won, Who Lost in Media Coverage of Conflict." *Los Angeles Times*, March 1, 1991. Available online at http://articles.latimes.com/1991-03-01/news/mn-2269_1_gulf-war Accessed on April 20, 2018.

Schonfeld, Reese. *Me and Ted Against the World: The Unauthorized Story of the Founding of CNN*. New York: Cliff Street, 2001.

Schwarz, Jon. "A Short History of U.S. Bombing of Civilian Facilities." *The Intercept*, October 7, 2015. https://theintercept.com/2015/10/07/a-short-history-of-u-s-bombing-of-civilian-facilities/ Accessed on April 30, 2018.

Shales, Tom. "Saddam's TV Offensive." *Washington Post*, August 29, 1990. https://www.washingtonpost.com/archive/lifestyle/1990/08/29/saddams-tv-offensive/b3256fc9-b196-4481-a2fd-c91a4c814968/?utm_term=.ea06729cc813 Accessed on April 1, 2018.

Ted Turner. *Inside Philanthropy*, https://www.insidephilanthropy.com/glitzy-giving/ted-turner.html Accessed on April 8, 2018.

"Ted Turner Named Time's 'Man of the Year.'" UPI.com, December 28, 1991. https://www.upi.com/Archives/1991/12/28/Ted-Turner-named-Times-Man-of-the-Year/6522693896400// Accessed on April 22, 2018.

"This Is CNN's 30th Anniversary." Emmys.com, http://m.emmys.com/news/interviews-project-news/cnns-30th-anniversary Accessed on April 20, 2018.

"Trump to CNN Reporter: You Are Fake News." CBNC, January 11, 2017. https://www.cnbc.com/video/2017/01/11/trump-to-cnn-reporter-you-are-fake-news.html Accessed on May 8, 2018.

Index

About the Author

Michael Burgan is a freelance writer who specializes in books for children and young adults, both fiction and nonfiction. A graduate of the University of Connecticut with a degree in history, Burgan is also a playwright and the editor of *The Biographer's Craft*, the newsletter for Biographers International Organization. He lives in Santa Fe, New Mexico.